Where's Jukie?

Poems

A n d y   J o n e s

&

Essays

K a t e   D u r e n

Absurd Publications
Davis, California
www.thecaliforniaoddity.com

ISBN: 978-0-9881772-1-5

Acknowledgement is made to journals in which some of these poems
previously appeared:

Split Stock: "The Time of the Rubber Duck"
Blue Moon Literary and Art Review: "What Jukie Might Be Thinking"
originally published as "Directives"
The Oddity: "The Death of Lillian" "Fever" "Low Tide"

Online Publication:

Thriving in Holland: http://kateduren.blogspot.com

Cover:

"Anatomy in Four Pieces" created by Eino81

Authors' Note: All profits from the sales of the book *Where's Jukie?* will be
donated to the Smith-Lemli-Opitz Foundation to fund medical research into
the causes, treatment, and understanding of Smith-Lemli-Opitz syndrome.

for Jackson

"I'll speak to thee in silence."

– William Shakespeare
Cymbeline

Contents

Poems

Essays

My Entropy Elephant

He is my entropy elephant, my kangaroo of chaos.
The contents of all drawers will be revealed!
All shirts become T-shirts! All gowns strapless!
If a tree falls in the forest, run to take the axe from his hands.
If the water main has broken, then he has taken a break;
water seeks its own level, and this boy is a guide!
Left-handed people are sinister and clumsy, they say.
Well our little lefty hoorays the lightning strike, the wind shear.
We get no rest from this tempest. The nanny cries.
It's not their stuff, so the neighbors just sit back and watch,
thinking, "With that arm he could pitch for the Giants."
"I never knew that pliers could be used in that way."
We can find no matches for his socks, his shoes, his mittens.
He plays with matches; how will we ever find him a match?

Meet Jukie

Meet Jukie. Probably more than any other photo I have, this one shows Jukie's true self. Yes, he is sitting inside a box on the top shelf of his closet. Yep, that box is dangerously close to falling off that shelf. Notice the artful balancing act with his right foot. Jukie lives on the edge. He's never happier than when teetering on the brink – the edge of a high shelf, a rooftop at midnight, or the limit of his mom's patience.

We're used to the quizzical looks from strangers: Jukie calls attention to himself. You can't miss the bright red chewy set of keys dangling from his mouth. He's got a shriek like a fire engine to match his red hair. And he's the fastest kid you'll ever see whiz past. Passersby usually display the same facial expression, which seems to say, "What's with that kid??" Smith-Lemli-Opitz syndrome is what. SLO is one of those rare syndromes that no one's ever heard of, including myself before we learned of Jukie's diagnosis. It means that Jukie cannot metabolize cholesterol the way that everyone else does. (It turns out, cholesterol is extremely important to every cell in the body.) Since he is non-verbal, Jukie communicates with pictures (Picture Exchange Communication System), gestures, and kisses. Because he gets extremely frustrated, Jukie sometimes bites and screams.

One day, my daughter Geneva said to me, "You know, we're kinda like The Incredibles!" I loved that, because I knew exactly what she meant. Our home calls for superhero parenting. Secretly, I think of regular ol' parents as sort of civilians. One's relationship with Jukie requires more–than–typical patience, empathy, kindness, and sometimes even sacrifice. And in this way, Jukie gives back; we all have more patience, kindness, and empathy for everyone. Jukie makes us all better.

I'm not sure how many times I've heard it from friends and strangers alike, but I'd guess it's well into the 100's – some version of "Jukie is really lucky to have you guys." People mean well, and I know that's true.

We love, love, love our boy and give him all that we have to give. But, honestly, I truly feel that we are the lucky ones to have been given such a special spirit, all wrapped in an adorable red-headed package. I feel as if I know secrets that most don't know. And I am so incredibly grateful – for all of it.

Having a special child means that you have a forever changed lens through which you view the world. I take just about nothing for granted, and value almost everything. Every small stride Jukie makes, everything the other kids do, each struggle that I have – I appreciate all of it! Jukie brings a spirit of innocence and purity into our lives (mixed with plenty of chaos as well, of course), which I feel honored to receive. Oddly enough, I am in a perpetual state of gratitude.

Warm Bottle

The warm bottle promises
but fleeting relief
from a mother's
perceived attack –
the pain
of her absence,
the pain
of her absent breast
growing black
in his stomach, spreading
quick like scalding water;
his limbs lurch independent
of his attempts to control them:
small uprisings in the high chair,
piteous rebellions from the mahogany crib.
The bottle fills and empties, fills and empties:
it confuses the heart.

Fever

Five in the morning.
I should have no reason to know
that it is light at this hour.
The roar of San Francisco
-bound commuters
past my Vacaville apartment
makes everything tremble,
and reminds the birds that they
too can start their engines.
My personal alarm keeps
going off, over and over.
Sometimes as I stumble past
the hallway clock I am surprised
by how little time has passed
since my last stumble.
Nobody sleeps.
Jukie's fever cuts
with desperate cries,
his nerves afire with jolty
pain: exposed fear
in shortened breaths. Suddenly
dark now in the shaded room,
I listen for life deep in the crib,
and then I reach for the heat.

Scarecrow

Amid the cornrows,
every third step is a stumble.
He winks at the crows
who circle above him.
Three years old,
he thinks of chocolate
while hugging as much
corn as he can,
as if being painted
by Diego Rivera.
My lawn chair is shaded
by the oak tree's tallest branches.
Eating pomegranates
and sipping seltzer water,
I track my son
via the rustling,
via the laughter.

Jukie Magic

Imet my husband Andy while we were both studying abroad in London. Even though we were only 20 years old, we talked about big life stuff. Andy told me, "I'm going to marry you someday." I responded, "I'm destined to have a child with special needs." How did I know? I just knew. Twenty-two years later, I've experienced enough Jukie magic to wonder if Jukie had been preparing me for what would become my greatest spiritual journey. As it turns out, I believe that this prior intuition, these messages from some challenging and mystical future, helped me to accept my eventual arrival in what parents of children with special needs know as "Holland" in 2001 – the year Jukie was born.

Was my intuition in fact Jukie whispering to me in my dreams, letting me know he was getting ready to join our family? The month before he was conceived, I told Andy, "A boy is coming." I'm glad I said it out loud, or I might wonder if this Jukie magic was indeed acting upon me. Throughout the pregnancy, we didn't find out the baby's gender; we wanted the surprise. But I informed everyone that he was a boy because he had already told me.

Jukie's birth was beautiful – in a tub underwater, with no drugs. I "caught" him myself, scooped him into my arms, and sat with him in the warm water. We looked silently into each other's eyes for a long time. Little did I know that such looks would be our primary mode of communication for many years to come.

Our tiny Jukie Buddha looked a little like Yoda. He had

droopy eyelids and wise, expressive eyes. As he grew in the first year, I came to see that Jukie was different from other babies in both appearance and behavior. When we learned of his SLO diagnosis ten months after he was born we thought we had found an answer, the solution to Jukie.

Obviously, no parent wants to hear that her child looks the way s/he does because of some mysterious and unheard-of syndrome. I wanted Jukie's droopy eyes, his ptosis, to be *Jukie's* look, not the SLO look. For a while, I refused to believe that Jukie would be anything other than a typical kid. We weren't always helped by the experts' optimism, and the oft-repeated belief that with his scores and advantages, Jukie was unlike any other child with SLO. "He'll go to UC Davis, rather than Stanford," one geneticist said. No one recommended Early Intervention services. With such encouragement, we moved willingly into sanguine denial and lived there a good year and a half.

So, if I knew in my teens that I was going to have a special kid, why was it such a struggle for me to accept Jukie's diagnosis? Acceptance is still a process, and a long one. I don't know another parent of a child with a disability, no matter how hopeful she might be, who didn't struggle in the beginning. The short Emily Perl Kingsley essay, "Welcome to Holland," written in 1987 (the year Andy and I met), helps give us one perspective on this journey.

When it came to understanding Jukie, those early experts were no experts, but a mom knows, doesn't she? Moms are the first to recognize something going on with their babies. And this is how it was for us. I saw that none of the specialists' or teachers' predictions were accurate.

Jukie was on an entirely different path from the one we were imagining for him. He wasn't even on the same map! And eventually, as all of this became clear, we moved from denial right into despair. That was the period of time when we went into "fix Jukie" mode. Poor Jukie. Undoubtedly, he sensed our deep aching for him to change course. And it was around this time that

I had a revelatory dream:

Andy, Geneva, Jukie and I are driving down a winding road that becomes more and more frightening as the road buckles and loops like a roller coaster. We struggle to keep our wheels on the pavement. There is no map in the car. We have no idea where we're going. And then a voice says, "Ask Jukie. He knows the way."

Wow. More Jukie magic. Just when life felt impossible, Jukie stepped in. It's probably been five years since I had this dream. And I think about it all the time. Not surprisingly, people often ask where Jukie got his nickname. We have always credited his sister Geneva for naming him, as we first heard it from her. But, is it possible that Jukie whispered in her ear?

Here's the thing. Jukie can't talk. He resists eye contact. His little body is more fragile than ours. He faces many challenges every day. Nevertheless, he usually seems to be the wisest person in the room. When the rest of us are running around the house, stressing about this or that, we'll often look over to find him quietly watching us, a bemused smile on his sweet face. And then the Jukie magic strikes. As we stop what we're doing and focus on Jukie, he showers us with kisses as if to say, "Slow down. It will all be *ok*."

It took me several years to figure out that Jukie often mirrors my feelings, rather than my mask. Sometimes he will burst into the shrieks that communicate his otherworldly sensitivity, as if to scream, "I'm feeling your stress, Mom!" And so, Jukie teaches us to slow down. Jukie wants nothing more than to run around and play, to eat yummy food, to take a warm bath, to have a good laugh, to give some sweet kisses, and to spend time with the people he loves.

And truly, isn't that what life's all about?

Spirit in the Alfalfa

For Tito (1967 – 1993)

If I cannot hear you,
it is because you have blown
ahead of me,

running and dodging
in the alfalfa,
functionally invisible,

free now of blood,
free now of restriction,
the borders we delighted in,

and still remembering me,
inhabiting all our memories,
if only once more

before broadening like an equator,
enlarging impossibly,
like the intimacy of God.

Flowers in Winter

Nothing slows me more
during the weight of winter storms
than the memory of flowers

whose only desire and chore
was to remain desirously firm
amid the sun and showers;

such thoughts of sublime rapport
still thrill me as I wait, and still warm
me during these unmoving winter hours.

Dinner

When I get up from the table,
you cry.
Our relationship is the most honest.

Sometimes with the spoon,
sometimes with the napkin,
I wipe the applesauce from your chin.

The crow caws to us
from the backyard.
You crane your neck to see.

At dinnertime your fingers
are dull tools.
You swat at the spoon.

Feeling gravity too keenly,
you sink into the chair.
You must be strapped in.

You look at me as if to speak.
Your eyes refocus before
you chirp like a hyena.

The wasps thump against the screen.
How they wish the door
were thrown open.

Sometimes your mouth opens
so wide that I think you could roar.

The wind shifts the vertical blinds.
You look at them and cry.
How I wish I could understand you.

Three Kids and IKEA

After lunch, I put three crying kids in the car, trying to sound cheery, hoping my manic frivolity would rub off on them. "We're going to IKEA! Hey, we'll check out the toys, and then we'll eat some of their famous apple pie and chocolate cake. It'll be great!" Geneva was crying because I made her brush her hair. Truman was crying because I forgot to let him open the garage door. And Jukie was crying because his brother and sister were crying.

They'll feel better when we get to IKEA, I reassured myself.

Things started off well enough. Jukie tolerated riding in the shopping cart for a while. Truman had no patience for the cart, and he usually does less damage to the stores we visit, so I sprung him as we got off the elevator. Soon he was running like a junior sprinter through the housewares, the Swedish offices, and amid the flimsy colorful furniture.

I found the long line I had to wait in to order our new desk while Geneva occupied Truman by spinning him in the office chairs. This isn't too bad, I'm thinking. I can handle this trip.

Then it started.

Jukie became less patient with the ride in the cart and started chucking his set of keys at passersby while sharing his signature Jukie shriek (think monkey crossed with a hyena). Truman started venturing farther and farther away, trying to lose his personal security guard. Then Jukie started with the shoes. Jukie hates shoes, he feels that they are unfairly restrictive. To show his displeasure with the slow-moving line and with his mobile IKEA cage, Jukie reverted to a practice favored by many Iraqi journalists: throwing his shoes at human targets.

I pretended that I understood what he meant by this sandal shot put, and let him out of the cart. Holding Jukie's shoes and my tongue, I stepped away from the cart for a moment to watch the boys run amok in different directions, happy not to hear anything breaking. How do the fates repay me for this maternal diligence? Someone stole our cart – the cart with the information about the desk I ordered (and the purpose of our waiting in line).

I reassigned Geneva to watch Truman while I dragged Jukie all over looking for the malefactor who took our precious cart.

Jukie didn't like the cart, but he really didn't like this new journey or the feeling of my Kung-Fu grip on his wrist, so he started taking bites out of my hand while trying to keep up with me. Soon the other shoppers were wondering why this woman was dragging a screaming child with her as she examined their carts.

I let Jukie go for just a moment in order to get back, again, into the line to order the desk. After a split second, Jukie took off and crashed into the only person in the whole of IKEA with more sensitive ears than Jukie's. Jukie ran headlong into a blind man. I got there just in time to apologize and keep Jukie from stealing the man's cane.

I looked around to see if anyone else was noticing the tragi-comedy unfolding when I caught a glimpse of Truman standing on top of a train table. Emulating his big brother, he had stolen someone's roll of wrapping paper and was bashing light fixtures with it. In a stroke of genius, I stowed Jukie in a crib – another cage for our wild child – while I collected Truman.

I tried to reassert the manic cheeriness that we started with in the minivan. "It's time for a treat break, everyone! Let's go find that pie and cake I promised you!" Maybe I shouldn't have been surprised that the dessert shelves were empty. The woman behind the counter told me that all of the pieces of cake and pie were frozen. Of course they are. Whatever. I told her that I would take one of each.

The kids were such a handful in line that a nice woman behind me took pity and told me that she is a mother of four, three of them boys, and that she knows what it's like to deal with unruly children. Of course, I thought, unless you have a Jukie, you really can't know, but she's sweet and empathic and I enjoyed a momentary reprieve from my stress with a nice conversation. In response to this mom's comment about Jukie's beautiful red hair, I looked down and saw that Jukie had taken his shoes and socks off. Again. While I was bending down to put them back on, the woman arrived with our frozen pie and cake. She didn't see me so she took the confections back to the huge freezer in the kitchen.

As I stood up, Geneva filled me in on what happened, so I started waving my arms wildly saying, "I'm over here! I'm the woman who wants the frozen dessert!" Oh. My. God. Is this really my life? It's like I'm Lucille Ball.

While we were waiting to pay for our frozen treats, Truman started screaming with sudden outrage that he was not the one to put the food on the tray: "I wanted to do it. I wanted to put dat on dere."

Jukie's shoes are off again.

We headed over to the closest table where Geneva boxed Jukie into the booth so I could gather our requisite ton of napkins and silverware. I arrived back to the table in time to witness Truman attempt to carry the frozen chocolate cake to his spot at the table. Thanks to lightening quick reflexes (developed primarily during Jukie's life), Geneva and I each caught a section of the cake, thus preventing it from landing in Truman's lap as his plate tipped vertically.

As I searched for my Excedrin Migraine in my purse, I watch Truman forget that we don't tip cups while drinking through straws. Juice fills his lap. More crying.

Somehow I chose to wear a shirt that was the same shade of yellow as those worn by the army of IKEA employees. As we checked out, every shopper in the Sacramento Valley asked me for directions, for advice, and for translations of the capitalized Swedish words on their potential purchases. With a boy under each arm, I wanted to scream, "Do I look like I work here?!"

Of course, I did.

At the self-service checkout, nothing scans. I wondered if that anti-depressant I took this morning was just a placebo.

On our way out, Truman insisted on riding one of those huge flat carts – the ones with the wheels that go in every direction – with Geneva as the driver. Jukie jumped on, too, and soon the chorus of screams parted the exiting crowd, like cars making way before the sirens of an ambulance.

The Functional Family

I.
Questions from Geneva, Age Eight

Daddy, the new *APR* is here! Does it have any of my poems?
Daddy, who is the protagonist of this story? What is the climax?
Is that an obstacle? Do all the obstacles come from the antagonist?
Could I have some cotton candy?
What if bad-guys stole my personality?
Could we catch their getaway car?
Could we crack their safes?

Jukie, you are un-helping me.
Daddy, you are being un-responsible with your very own kids!
Daddy, don't wake the Teletubbies!
Don't disturb the Wiggles!
Daddy, do you see a truck?
Do you see a truck?
Daddy, what if you wrote an entire poem using only my words?

II.
Jackson

We get many first invitations to family dinners, but never seconds.

One neighbor had wall-to-wall carpeting until Jackson came for a visit.

One had no-wax floors until Jackson taught him about wax.
"Behold," he said in his Jukie way, "I present to you 100 varieties of wax!"
Wineglass in hand, the husband led me from the playroom
as Jukie balanced atop the terrarium, reaching for the candles.
It's his house, I thought, and we'll be gone soon.
Soon the floor was a variegation of wax!
Behold the candle wax, earwax, beeswax and mix of wine and cheese wax!

Jesse Jackson once said that America is not a blanket –
one piece of unbroken cloth, the same color,
the same texture, the same size.
No, Jesse taught us that America is more like a quilt –
many pieces, many colors, many sizes,
all woven and held together by "a common thread."
Finally quiet in his crib, but never asleep,
our Jackson has found that common thread,
and he has pulled it hard.
Behold our quilt now.

The patterned symmetries are now scarred by acid rain.
The heads of the ducks and the rabbits have been clear-cut.
This land is his land.
That smog I smell has licked its tongue into the corners of our evenings!
Jackson, your storms and hurricanes have leveled the shelf of picture books.
Jackson, we still feel the effects of your tsunami.
Thunder lizard, joy buzzer, wordless banshee:
behold, it's Jackson!

III.
Truman's Section

Truman's section of the house he shares with the photo albums, the
    computer,
the guest bed, the Jackson-free toys (all precious, all breakable).
At four months, when not sleeping, this unsuspecting boy smiles broadly.
He lives to catch our eye.

At Geneva's show and tell, Truman is that which is shown.
"He could win a staring contest," said one boy.
We stare and stare at this last child, the blue boots,
the drool bib, the dragon jammies to which we have pinned our hopes.
We are counting on you, tiny child.
At 75th percentile weight, 90th percentile height,
your size matches both siblings together at this age.
Good for you boy!
Grow strong legs, for at times you will need to run.
Your hands now can palm a ping-pong ball;
soon that broad grip will block less gentle projectiles.
Those soft shoulders, now so close to your ears,
will broaden, strengthen, and calcify
under loads we are thankful not to imagine.

Low Tide

I was following Jukie
        as he hopped among the tide pools,
                causing havoc.
He picked up
        and sometimes picked apart
                what he could find:
seaweed,
        fragile shells,
                rough and leathery starfish;
the tentacles
        and polyps
                of sea anemone.
I imagined him
        a nuclear beast,
                roaring incomprehensibly:
someone that Godzilla,
        hero mammoth,
                might take on.
Soggy little villagers,
        I can almost hear
                your screams.
I spied an octopus,
        but didn't show it to him,
                this wanton boy.

Such a destroyer.
        I hope the ocean is safe
                this far from Japan.
I will protect my monster,
        his blood as salty
            as the sea,
from whatever
        oversized nuclear tentacles
             may reach for him.
Must I also protect
        the worlds, the stars,
            which he would destroy?

Jukie and the Dead

> "Whatever your life's work is, do it well. A man should do his job so well that the living, the dead, and the unborn could do it no better."
>
> – Martin Luther King, Jr.

Grand-Davey and Jukie are sitting together on the couch.
He doesn't know that his grandfather is, as the newspaper says, "famed."
A graduate student has devoted a dissertation to Davey's life's work.
Together they counted (and recounted) that he had directed a thousand plays.
He would die on Jukie's thousandth day.

Ptosis Jukie tips over beholding giant Grand-Davey in the hat.
He likes the colors of the necktie, and the jangly keys.
He wants to remove the hat from the loud man's head.
He wants to shake the hat, and pull the string,
and taste the brim.

I have to tell my Dad that Jukie isn't getting better.
On Thanksgiving, we arrive with a pharmacy, and nebulize him thrice daily.
I don't know that he ever will get married, Dad. This is now my work.
The geneticist says he'll never attend Stanford.
Poppycock, Grand-Davey proclaims, projecting like an actor.

Everybody but Jukie knows that Grand-Davey is dying,
and the visitors keep coming, mostly method actors. Nobody cries.
Grand-Davey will say no to the morphine, but later relent.
Someone will suggest *Beauty and the Beast* while he rests.
Nana learns how to smoke outside.

Later Jukie will drop Nana's camera into her coffee.

Jukie Antics

"You should write a book." I hear this often. Everyone seems to think there's a book to be written about life with Jukie. His antics are practically Davis legend. Jukie's hijinks are both so maddening and entertaining that they've made for many a humorous party story. "You'll laugh or you'll cry," we are told. Only, I don't have to look hard to find the humor. Jukie's pretty damn funny. I mean, who else but Jukie would get into a tug-o-war with a 90-year-old with her own cane?

Jukie's chaos started early. As soon as he was up and walking he was pulling stunts like dunking his Nana's camera into her coffee. Soon we discovered that he'd often announce his plans with a fiendish laugh. When the room is still and Jukie giggles to himself out of context... look out! And if he's laughing maniacally as we tuck him into bed, we know it's going to be a long night.

When he was three years old, Jukie dragged a chair across his nursery school classroom over to the fish tank. Then he grabbed a teapot from the housekeeping area, climbed up on the chair, and scooped the fish out pouring them all over the counter. When I arrived at school to pick him up, his teacher announced, "Jukie went fishing today!" (Thank God for those fabulous teachers over the years who love and "get" Jukie!) No water source is safe. Jukie. Loves. Water. Water table set out for play? Jukie will sit in it. Water sitting in a glass on the table? Jukie will pour it all over the newspaper.

One of Jukie's mottos is "Why walk, when I can run?" As with all children with SLO, Jukie's motor skills were delayed. Unlike most of his SLO buds, Jukie learned to walk at 17 months and learned to *run* almost immediately thereafter. When I say run, I do mean *run*. He runs everywhere. And he's fast. His psychiatrist (at Kennedy Krieger Institute/Johns Hopkins, and an SLO expert) says that Jukie is the most hyperactive child she has ever met. Ever. Jukie has scaled our eight-foot fence and run a mile away from home (sans shoes or shirt). After a 911 call and frantic search, he was located at a favorite park, playing happily in the sand. Only Jukie could manage to run headlong into a blind man and steal *his* cane (see the IKEA story – clearly, Jukie has a thing for canes).

Perhaps because he's so small for his age, Jukie continually surprises others with his speed. At Costco once, Jukie sat in the shopping cart watching the employee ring up our purchases. As soon as the cash drawer opened, Jukie reached down, grabbed all of the pennies and chucked them up in the air as hard as he could so that they rained down upon our heads. Even if I had known what he was planning, I'd have struggled to stop him with his lightning-quick speed. He's also got excellent evasive moves. You'd think that he, rather than his sister, had been studying Tae Kwon Do for years when you watch him expertly escape my grip on his wrist and flee – all in one swift move. There are many times when I'm no match for my crafty running boy.

Jukie could climb before he could walk; climbing is his thing.

Like a cat, he prefers to perch up high. When he was born, his droopy eyelids (known as ptosis) prevented him from seeing much of the world. It was as if he were always wearing a hat with a brim down low over his eyebrows. Climbing enabled Jukie to see the world. Jukie is resourceful and figured that out early. So we let him. We provide as many high spaces as we can for our boy to get his climbing fix. But, he had one more space in mind. A few months back, we heard a knock at our door. Who could it be at 11:30 PM? It was our neighbor, out walking his dog, who noticed Jukie running around on our roof. Our *roof*. Jukie had managed to open his window, rip off his screen, and climb out and onto the roof. There may not be an accomplishment for which Jukie feels more pride. He knew exactly what he wanted to do, and figured out a way to do it.

The time he ran away, I had previously told him that we were not going to the park, which he had requested through PECS. So, he climbed the fence and took himself.

The most successful explorers have always had more bravery and curiosity than sense. Jukie is our little Magellan.

Seven Steps to Heaven

"I'm always thinking about creating. My future starts when I wake up in the morning and see the light."

– Miles Davis

Ours is an unhurried August Saturday morning.
My wife is visiting Chicago for a fortnight,
while Miles Davis fills the kitchen.

The trumpet croons. How can something so cool, born in 1957, be so old?
The title of our chosen British underground internet radio station,
"Giants of Jazz Radio," seems more oxmoronic with every passing moment,
but here we are, dancing like oxymorons.
The bulldog dances too, yelping, and nipping at our legs,
wondering what strange game we are playing.

When I told Truman that for the next three weeks
we would dance to jazz anytime we felt compelled to reach for the remote,
he gave me a high five.
No one will stop us from acting rashly.

Reminiscent of last night's dinner, today's breakfast is made up of appetizers,
many plastic bowls full of cereal, raisins, walnuts, fruit slices and trail mix
that we carry with us, if we want, into the back yard –
the screen door left comfortably open.

Atop the treehouse, Jukie's rhythms are slow-moving and harmonic,
a groaning modal jazz that the neighbors now know by heart.
The cicadas provide him a chorus.
Every summer day for him is a Saturday.

Until he finds the four to six Crocs
he's hidden in the bushes, or thrown over the fence, he will go barefoot.
Luckily, his feet are almost as big as his mom's,
and she left us a sea of shoes.

I see half-read *New Yorkers*, the bowls of raisins,
art projects, the distributed detritus of pruned leaves and vines,
and the bulldog now sprawled across the picnic table.
Our yard is a closed ecosystem
of idyllic inattention and practiced caprice.
Nobody will spy us here in our boxers, jammies, and yesterday's t-shirts.

Somewhere around here is my list of chores.
I've fed the dog and distributed medications,
but I haven't yet touched the laundry or the dishes.
As Miles would say, "So what?"

Getting Attention

I spun and spun like that
because I wanted to get high,
and I whacked the world
a thousand times
with my plastic bat
because I wanted to test
the world's hollowness,
and I also wanted to test
my body's resilience,
and my relationship with pain,
and the limits of my extremities,
and to see
if gravity
cared
that I had an umbrella in each hand,
or that I wore a cape.

Gravity didn't care
and the hollow bat didn't care
and I had trouble finding a person,
even a parent,
who really cared,
who understood and cared.

But the pain I found was real,

and if I concealed my wounds, they were mine only,
and nobody asked about the blood,
and nobody asked about the limp,
and I went for almost a week before relenting,
descending the stairs in tears,
cradling my elbow,
screaming that it was time,
it was time,
it was time for the
ambulance,
and that if somebody didn't hurry,
I might just die.

Second Family

By the time Jukie was diagnosed with Smith-Lemli-Opitz syndrome at twelve months of age, we had already spent one year with our "typical" baby. He was going to grow up, go to college, get married, and probably have a family of his own. And before that, he was going to play on a soccer team, attend his big sister Geneva's school, and experience the childhood that everyone takes for granted. Instead, just before his first birthday, we learned that he was born with a serious and rare genetic disorder called Smith-Lemli-Opitz Syndrome (or SLO).

Wow.

It was Thanksgiving weekend when we got the phone call; we were in Las Vegas to spend the holiday with family. In shock, I tucked that news into a compartment in the back of my mind. And the genetic team encouraged us to live in this compartmentalized denial. They told us that Jukie was so unusual for the syndrome that it made no sense for us to learn anything about it. And if the specialists thought I should bask in denial, who was I to argue? I could ignore devastating news if that's what was asked of us. And it was – and so I did.

After a few months, I slowly started to realize that the medical team was wrong. Jukie was seriously impacted by this syndrome, and we had to face it. I started building a community and a system of support. I began regularly meeting for dinners with other moms of kids with disabilities. I loved getting to know these women, and found sharing stories, hopes, and fears immeasurably helpful.

But something was missing – the other parents of kids with Jukie's diagnosis. SLO is so rare that there are only a handful of (known) families touched by the syndrome in each state. The problem was that I didn't feel that we belonged in that community. In just about every way, Jukie was unusual, for, unlike other kids with his syndrome, he was meeting most of his developmental milestones.

I thought that the other SLO families would have a hard time accepting Jukie. And, honestly, I was afraid that contact with families whose kids weren't doing as well might depress me. Everything changed when I received a phone call from Fargo, North Dakota. A woman named Gretchen had read something I had written in a newsletter for SLO families about Jukie. I could hear the agony in her voice. She thought that her son Markie might have what Jukie has. I heard a kindred spirit and loved this woman instantly. In some odd way, I felt as if we had known each other forever.

We talked for hours. Even though the Mayo clinic had told Gretchen that Markie didn't have SLO, she and I consulted with each other as two laypeople, two mothers, and concluded that he likely did.

Markie was tested again, and this time was positive for SLO. And that's when my life started turning in a new direction.

Gretchen and I talked endlessly on the phone, giggled about our silly similarities, nicknamed each other "Toots," and understood each others' lives like no one else could. In cahoots with my husband Andy, Toots flew out to California to surprise me and visit for a long weekend. We hugged and cried in the street when we met. It felt like meeting a long-lost sister. Family. And somewhere down our lineage, we truly are family, for Markie and Jukie both have a rare mutation of SLO that only two others in the world are known to share.

Four years ago, I didn't know anyone other than Jukie who had SLO. Today, I know many, and cannot imagine where I would be without them, without my SLO family. We know. Nothing needs to be said, no explanations are necessary to understand each other. I feel as though all of the kids with SLO are nieces and nephews to me, and cousins to one another. Any of us would do absolutely anything for another SLO family member. And we speak shorthand.

I once sent an email to Toots mentioning a concern that I had about Jukie. The phone rang not five minutes later – at 11:00 PM. Toots sensed my anxious mood and knew to call, and I burst into tears the moment I heard her voice. Technology enables us to participate in each other's lives so much more than ever before. We follow the kids' and each other's daily lives as if we were all just down the street from one another. So when Melissa writes that Carson is finally taking the bus to school again after a long hiatus following foot surgery, we cheer him on, knowing the struggle to get there. When Blossom isn't herself, I worry about her health AND the sanity of her mama, Lotus, who is home taking care of her. I wait for pictures of Blossom smiling again, and know when I finally see happy photos, that things are better.

Jukie will never read this, this record of our Jukie discoveries and hopes. And although that Thanksgiving phone call all those years ago was difficult to answer, it's not hard to remind myself that I so appreciate the lessons Jukie and his SLO cousins have taught me. Who could have predicted that such a little guy would have so widened my world?

Portrait of Boy

I am packed solid like a double cone.
No wind passes through my clothes,
for I am impermeable, hermetically sealed.
Nothing green here except the far pines,
and the lettering on my flexible flyer.
I am inflexible, perched at the top
of an impossibly long slope,
unable to move, wary even of looking around.
I hear hoof beats on a snow day
while the world vanishes one snowflake at a time.
At the bottom, I can almost make out my sister.
Her overcoat a drop of red upon an inconceivable canvas.
Blinking away a tear, I seize with potential energy
and cannot let go of my sled.

Spilled Fennel in Faneuil

Uncomfortable, squarish, hardscrabble,
hungry Henry Tippet tripped on the tinsel,
and jolted into fandango, a dangerous shuffle,
an ungentle joggle, awkward, inadmissible;
spinning counter-clockwise amid the truffles,
chestnut pies, gold coins spilled in the temple,
spent fennel, he up and peeled off in Faneuil Hall,
where Paul Revere smithed silver,
where he stood watchful with wary rifle,
and stands today an unweary sentinel,
mythic colonel fixed in black marble,
still as death above the slowing people
gasping and pointing amid the spilled fennel,
amid the grasping, tripping tinsel,
as Henry Tippet, dynamic but unjoyful,
spins there unleashed, unkenneled,
mistaken once as an unsought example
of merely the minutely "poor people,"
he now jerks free in the Christmas temple
unleashed now like a counterexample,
clearly uncoupled, perversely unpoliceable,
he is both simple and anything but simple.

What Jukie Might be Thinking

When you give me pants to wash, check the pockets first for Kleenex.
I've told lies that have traveled around the world before I put my pants on.

When you are done with the sports section, just recycle it – you
    know I'm not going to read it.
Aristotle's theater of pity and fear is recycled hourly in the gut of a poet.

If you see toys on the floor and are done playing with them, pick them up.
Each of man's lost toys reminds me that we have no home.

Whenever you go upstairs just ask yourself "What needs to go up?"
*The villain is like a man on a see-saw: he moves upwards and
    then down.*

Watch how I test the temperature of the milk in the bottle on the
    inside of my wrist.
*The watch on the wrist of the dead soldier moves at the same speed
    as mine.*

Water the groundcover every day in the summer, or it will all die.
The sweltering summer tells us to give thanks that all is ephemera.

No Small Victory

Often my life feels like a series of small victories. Mothering three young children requires a lot of negotiations. And while I hope for win-win scenarios where the kids and I feel equally satisfied, in the end, I'm still looking for victories. One benefit I've learned from my 12 years of parenting is which battles to pick.

As soon as the alarm sounds (usually four-year-old Truman climbing in bed next to me, laying his hand on my cheek and whispering, "Mommy, are you awake?"), the quest for victory begins.

We start with three kids to get out the door to three different schools at three different times. I cross my fingers that picking out their clothes will be smooth. It seems that Truman only wants to wear stripes, and of course no striped clothes are clean! "Maybe just for today, you can wear a dump truck shirt," I offer. Geneva, who is twelve years old, has an aversion to most socks. They never "feel good on her feet." So, I hope that each morning her socks will go on her feet without my hearing about it. And as a family we negotiate with and overcome these sorts of obstacles all day long. What? Truman thought that it was his turn to close the garage door? More negotiations ensue. Next time, Little Man. What? You don't have to go to the bathroom? Well, we're going on a three-hour car trip, so how about you get in there and use the potty anyway.

Of course, I've learned the fine art of giving the kids the illusion of choice. When they're young, it's: "Do you want to drink from a blue cup or a red cup?" Either way, they're drinking what I've chosen. With the oldest, it's: "Would you like a sleepover Friday or Saturday night?" The goal was one sleepover night, not two, as would otherwise have been requested.

And with my sweet, special Jukie, victories are non-stop. Much of my time with Jukie involves simply trying to control the chaos while allowing him as much freedom as possible. We've put a lot of thought and energy into exploring how we as a family can coexist happily, with as many win-win outcomes as possible. And when I'm on Jukie-duty, the negotiations are active and constant. As a result, I rarely sit down at home.

Who needs a gym?

Perhaps these constant tiny battles prepare me well for the big ones. A few weeks ago, I went to war against Jukie's county regional center, Alta California Regional Center. In California, budgets everywhere are depleted, so perhaps we should not have been surprised when Alta informed us that they would no longer be funding Jukie's "Care Trak" monitoring system: an ankle bracelet that emits a radio signal so that Jukie can be tracked by the local police department everywhere he goes.

Jukie has a history of running away. Ergo, this ankle bracelet is vital.

After telling us that they were planning to cancel support for the program (which a local activist and mom raised the money to initiate), Alta offered a series of silly compensatory suggestions: "Why not install an elevated lock on the front door?" "Had we tried 'behavior modification'?" "What about 'direct supervision'?" Gee, why didn't we think of any of those!

Anyone who spends even five minutes with Jukie can see how able a climber he is, and how easily he would have defeated that front door lock tactic (which he began to do in preschool). And behavior modification? We've been modifying Jukie's behavior with the help of every professional we can enlist for nine years now. Alta's suggestion that "there is no substitute for direct supervision" felt like an especially cruel joke.

My husband, Andy, and I are human. We require sleep each night. Of course we directly supervise our boy every minute of the day. He even sleeps with a night-vision video monitor on his bed. With all of our vigilance, Jukie has still escaped – twice!

Round one: Andy and I met with Alta representatives for an "informal meeting" to try to come to a resolution without involving the courts. Because we believed that Alta would listen to our reasonable argument – that the agency should continue to fund the monthly cost of his ankle bracelet – we agreed to this meeting. This was a mistake we would not make again. Alta's legal consultant, their "impartial arbiter," acted as a judge. This didn't bode well, but the woman seemed friendly enough. We brought with us the coordinator of the Care Trak Program, a wonderful police officer. Along with us, she spoke of the necessity of Care Trak, and demonstrated the pings coming from her monitoring device, which belong solely to Jukie.

Did I mention that we brought Jukie? If the Alta folks were to understand our argument, they'd need to see and meet Jukie. Surely, they'd conclude that he needed to continue to be monitored through the Care Trak.

The meeting took about an hour, during which time Jukie ran around in circles, tried to climb the blinds, untied everyone's shoelaces, and ate from the trashcan.

You go, Jukie! Show them what'cha got! And let them see what a precious little boy you are, so worthy of tracking.

As we left the building that day, I said to Andy and to our trusty police officer, "I'd be shocked if they didn't rule in our favor." One week later, we heard Alta's decision. They did not rule in our favor. Did we still want to pursue this, they asked? I imagine that at this point many parents would understandably give up. These sorts of battles require large amounts of time, energy, and perseverance. Taking the matter to court before a judge can feel incredibly intimidating.

Did I want to pursue the matter? Absolutely! Pursue!

Round two: Once again, Andy, Jukie, our police officer and I reconvened, this time, sworn in, speaking into microphones, and before a judge. To our surprise, our Alta opposition was led by the "impartial arbiter" from our previous encounter. Now as prosecutor, she used against us every argument we made at our "informal" meeting.

Andy and I have no law background, unless you count watching an occasional trial on TV (hello OJ!). We thought we'd just be explaining ourselves directly to a judge. Instead, we found that our hearing would be conducted like a real court case, which, in retrospect, it was. Opening statements! Called witnesses! Cross examinations! Objections! Quickly realizing that Andy and I were out of our comfort zone (not to mention our league), we decided to step up and act the part. "How about I play lawyer, and you play witness," Andy whispered. Fortunately, Andy is a seasoned public speaker, quite used to running meetings. And of course I knew the ins and outs of our case. We could do it.

While Alta was presenting their case against us, I feverishly wrote down a long list of questions for my husband/lawyer to ask me.

Alta began making the case that because Jukie wears a Medi-cAlert bracelet, funding the Care Trak monitoring system would be a duplication of services. Again we heard about the importance of direct supervision. Our "friendly" prosecutor pointed out that I had turned down a referral for behavior modification, which she made sound, somehow, terribly irresponsible of me. We couldn't wait for our turn to speak! Soon enough, Andy was cross-examining Alta with fabulous questions, such as, "Is Jukie wearing a MedicAlert bracelet right now?" They couldn't say, for, as the woman from Alta was forced to admit, she could not see the bracelet under Jukie's sleeve. "If you saw Jukie sitting quietly, playing alone in the sand at a park, would you know immediately that he needed intervention?" he asked.

"No," she admitted, she would not.

We remember well that sitting alone and playing quietly in the sand was exactly what Jukie was doing when, a year earlier, he was found a mile from home at a favorite park. He had climbed our eight-foot fence!

When it was our turn to testify, I pointed out that the Medi-cAlert bracelet kicks in when Jukie is found. The Care Trak anklet is activated the moment he is lost. Jukie doesn't speak. He doesn't fear traffic or people or most any other danger he should. I told the judge that Jukie had proven his own case. He had already demonstrated the importance of tracking him. His police officer testified again.

The whole case went on for over two hours.

A funny thing happened when we left the court that day. I felt exuberant. Whatever happened, we felt as if we had already won. Andy and I came together over yet another obstacle. We found that we had enjoyed "playing lawyer" by reading each other's minds to make up for the absence of preparation (twenty-two years together helps). We stood up for (and with) Jukie and for all of the children in the county who use the Care Trak system.

I walked into the post office some time later and knew that the certified letter waiting there must be from the court.

Letter in hand, I ran back to my bike and decided to wait to open it until I arrived home. But I didn't make it home; I couldn't wait. Instead, I stopped at a bench on the Davis green-belt and ripped open the envelope. The first words I saw were, "claimant's appeal is granted." We won. Jukie won.

Yes, precious boy, you won. You are so worthy of tracking. I will follow you everywhere.

A Lateral Move

Oh to make a lateral move
into the next world,
corresponding, but just
different enough;

a world in which you
sit gratified in a barcalounger,
unburdened by television,
sipping pino grigio at dusk

by yourself, thinking thoughts
that others would pay,
in fact, do pay, for you to share.
An assistant deposits speaker's fees,

and finds and checks out new books,
and writes summaries, and rough drafts
of your correspondence, a collection
of which itself is to be published.

You are so static that you are almost
monumental, incapable of toppling.

Cell Story

Without slime we would have become nothing.
Moist and antediluvian fecundity
gave our splitting cells something to embrace,

a song to sing before there was music.
Green buds of goop took a billion years
to grow a brain and dexterous limbs.

Praise be to that crucial creature,
the bee, who added one stripe
every millennium, and soon provided color

to widen our palate. All the best predators
had their fun before we got here, takings risks
and eating creatures with long memories

who seemed willing to avenge the pain
upon us, screaming brachiators,
until the elephants knocked down our trees.

We stumbled blinking upon the savannah,
many of us to be quickly eaten so that
a few, you know the ones, could

express an analogous hunger, an urge
to imagine, to create, to make,
as they say, something out of our lives

as we continue to stir, and bring to a boil,
and add ingredients to, and perhaps solidify
that cell-remembered ubiquitous gloop.

Fulcra

The physics of fulcra
divide us, impose your
weight against mine,
but without touching,
keep me low when you're
high, keep you uninvolved
with my small victories.
I blame this distance,
this unstable, continuous
movement for my spiritual
vertigo, nausea in the absence
of God. Unforgiven, no perch
for prayer or even confession,
I sway and tilt and list with
one eye on you, one eye,
pleading and dilated, on the sky.

Sacred Classroom

This morning I sent my three children off to their three different schools. As I suspect every parent across America did, I kissed each of them a few extra times and hugged them longer and harder than on other mornings. Usually, I yell, "I love you – have a wonderful day...!" as they run or bike away from me. Today, I could hardly let them go as I paused for eye contact, this time asking, "Do you know how much I love you?" This morning wasn't like other mornings for this country seems to have forever changed since 20 impossibly beautiful and innocent six and seven-year-old children were slaughtered last Friday in their first grade classroom – a sacred place. Six heroic educators died trying to shield the children.

My youngest child (Truman) is a first-grader who attends a two-classroom K-3 school also located in an idyllic country setting. Truman turned seven in September. Last week, he finally lost that pesky front tooth that had been hanging on too long. Now he has that incredibly cute toothless gap which symbolizes first grade and, for me, has always represented the sweet innocence of the age. He believes in Santa and the Tooth Fairy. Other than the occasional conflict over Legos, he knows only peace and love in the world. As Andy and I discussed and debated how to approach our children with the news of Newtown, Connecticut, we could not imagine telling our boy that other first-graders were not safe in their classrooms. I remembered a conversation with Truman last summer as I was prepping him for a PG-rated animated film with some "bad guys." Wondering whether the movie would feel too scary for him to see, I said to him, "You know that all of the bad guys are only pretend...." He interrupted me with, "Of course I do, Mommy – bad guys aren't real; they don't really exist!" Had I been prepared for that response, I might have handled it differently. His innocence stunned and momentarily threw me. We were driving. I said nothing.

My middle child, Jukie, is 11 years old. I hope that he will only ever know peace and love in the world. Living always in the moment, Jukie loves and trusts everyone. Today, I am grateful to know his world. When I spend time with Jukie, I enter his reality. I lie in the backyard with him and watch the wind blow the leaves in the trees. I go through our routine of things-that-make-Jukie-laugh and watch him fall over with infectious Jukie giggles. I spin him on the tire swing. We sit and look eye to eye. I wonder what he is thinking and imagine that he is wondering the same about me. I will never have to tell him anything of the tragic events of last week.

Geneva, my oldest, is a sweet and thoughtful fifteen-year-old who currently straddles childhood and adulthood with tremendous grace. Sometimes I step back and watch her interact with others, marveling at the mature, composed young woman I see. Other times I find myself tending to grass stains on the knees of her jeans. As she is our firstborn, she is the child with whom we tried to get everything with parenthood "right." We protected her innocence by limiting media exposure and other worldly influences. We protected her little body by giving her only healthy food. I recall feeling a bit hesitant to introduce solid foods at the age of six months, for she had been exclusively breast-fed until that point. I realized that I wasn't always going to be able to control everything she ate. When she was in second grade she once asked me, "Mommy, have you ever used a curse word around me? And was I adjacent to you when you did?" Of course I remember this conversation perfectly, in part because I have been repeating and laughing about it ever since, and partly because those who know me well found this question a bit surprising. My brother jokingly commented at the time, "Wow – she doesn't really know you at ALL, does she?" All of this shielding came from wanting to believe that I could protect her from the world even as I knew I could not.

While our family stayed away from stories and images from Newtown over the weekend, I did watch the memorial service at which President Obama spoke. I think he spoke for every parent when he said this:

> *You know, someone once described the joy and anxiety of parenthood as the equivalent of having your heart outside of your body all the time, walking around....With their very first cry, this most precious, vital part of ourselves, our child, is suddenly exposed to the world, to possible mishap or malice, and every parent knows there's nothing we will not do to shield our children from harm. And yet we also know that with that child's very first step, and each step after that, they are separating from us; that we won't – that we can't – always be there for them.*

As much as I would like to believe in the illusion that I can keep my children safe at all times, I must admit that I can't always protect them. We parents cannot hold on so tightly that we don't allow our kids to go experience the world. Our job, after all, is to provide a solid foundation of love, nurturance, and protection when our children are young, so that they grow into competent, capable and independent young adults... who leave us – one of life's greatest ironies.

It so happened that before Geneva arrived home from school last Friday, she had heard about the shootings from a friend. Neither she nor I had discussed it with one another, each attempting to protect the other. Two days passed before I realized that she had already heard the terrible news. Truman knows nothing of the tragic event, and I have no plans to tell him. I will cross my fingers that he doesn't hear it from a classmate. Jukie will continue to hop on the school bus each morning, happily oblivious to any potential dangers. I will remind myself that the world is filled with love and beauty, that violence is the exception, and that I am doing my best to raise kind and generous children whose existence — and perhaps their bighearted naiveté — makes the world a better place.

Birthday Boy Wakes Early

The boy celebrates his birthday by waking early and throwing
   Legos at the twirling ceiling fan,
by doing handstands on the top shelf of his closet,
by putting on all his pajamas at once,
by removing the drawers from his dressers,
by removing the handles from his dresser drawers and then
   hiding the screws,
by bringing in the Sunday paper and reshuffling its pages,
by pouring three glasses of milk and forgetting where he has left them,
by eating fistfuls of Cranberry Macadamia Nut Cereal, right
   from the box,
by chasing the backyard scrub jays from their trees and bushes,
by stealing one line from this sonnet,
by testing the volume on the kitchen radio,
by removing from the walls all the pictures he can reach,
by greeting us finally at 7am with chocolate, a gift which he has
   already begun to share.

Sturm und Drang

Sad music,
once shared,
consoles through
headphones

the broken boy,
his studies
unstudied.
His sorrow

pricks him
frequently
with uneasy
delight.

Confections
scattered
in the dark
bedroom,

candy store
air mists
his bunk
with pink and green.

The Death of Lillian

Our neighbor with the windmills and the solar panels
didn't seem contrite that his hunting dogs
escaped his property for a chicken dinner.
The chickens were ours, and we loved them.
Jukie's sister, age ten, was brought in to identify
the carcasses, for only she could distinguish them.
The insurance man followed her with a pad of paper
around the huge coop, Geneva's second home.
Stiff-backed, dry-eyed and strong, the girl walked amid
The feathers and the blood, stopping often to point:
Rufous, Dante, Copernicus, Fresno, Johnny Wonderful,
Plinko, Flocko, Gladys, Mabel, Renfro, Higgins,
Memphis, Jerome, Jaleel, Mary-Kate, Fargo.
That one, Annabeth, was barren; we were preparing her for soup.
And this one, Lillian, she said, as she held up the body
for the man to see, Lillian would lay eggs only for me.

Love Unspoken

In the back of my closet, on the top shelf, is a box that I never open. I cannot. The ten-year-old videotapes inside it document the typical sorts of birthday parties, vacations, and holidays that every family records. I cannot bring myself to watch these particular videos for they happen to highlight the great heartbreak of my life: my son Jukie's loss of language.

Like many kids, Jukie's first word was "Mama." "Dada" quickly followed, as did his sister's nickname, "Oonie" (for "Boonie"), and his own name, "Ookie." Only those closest to Jukie grew to recognize his idiosyncratic pronunciation. One of my favorites, "Dee Dah Dohd" referred to his favorite Sesame Street character (Big Bird). Jukie delighted in sharing the names of favorite people and toys. Each afternoon as I plopped him in his car seat, he would chant, "Oonie an' Ellen, Oonie an' Ellen...!" because he knew that we were about to carpool with his sister and her best friend, Helen. His acquisition of language developed so slowly that we remarked on each word, learning along the way the Jukie version of each. I still remember the day he eagerly announced "Loon! Loon!" as we drove past a bouquet of balloons. And I clearly recall thinking excitedly that his language was finally starting to take off.

Looking back, I realize that the "loon" moment actually marked the peak of Jukie's linguistic bell curve. As slowly as he learned language, equally slowly did he lose those words he knew. At first he stopped identifying objects around the house.

Gradually he grew quieter and more serious. I assumed he was becoming more thoughtful. Then he stopped learning new words. I began to notice a decline in his use of familiar words, those that had brought with them such joy when first they appeared. Each dropped off one by one, and his vocabulary shrank.

One day I heard what would be his last "Ookie," and then his last "Dada." The final word he spoke was also his first. "Mama."

It is consoling to me that he held "Mama" until the end. And yet to consider that "Mama" was also his last word is, at times, almost too much to bear.

Looking back, I take comfort now in the many ways that Jukie and I have connected since the day I learned I was pregnant. I remember the delight of waiting until his birth for the surprise of his gender, yet still knowing that I was carrying a boy. ("Now you have one of each," said his grandfather, delightedly.) I think about the magic of his underwater tub birth, and of lifting him from the water and placing him on my chest. I remember the sweet intensity of his newborn gaze directly into my eyes – we knew each other instantly. I even marvel at his ability to nurse immediately (most kids with Smith-Lemli-Opitz syndrome never breast-feed), and feel gratitude that he and I shared that connection for a full year.

As Jukie grows, so does the complexity of his thoughts and actions. He communicates with us through a system of PECS (Picture Exchange Communication System) and sign language. For the most part, however, we have developed our own form of communication, which involves intuiting Jukie's needs and desires. As his experience of the world seems more visceral and emotional than logical or ego-based, he clues in to the emotions and energy of those closest to him. Much of our communication takes place in this exchange of energy and intuition – we can convey our messages simply by being together in silence. The instinctive nature of our relationship allows for and requires constant reciprocal connection. It depends upon gazes, caresses, hugs, and fleeting smiles. One afternoon, I overheard eight-year-old Truman's attempt at explaining our communication with Jukie to a new friend, "It's like Jukie's Chewbacca, and my sister's Han Solo." The *Star Wars* copilot analogy was perfect: We understand Jukie, and he understands us.

Parents know that children are our best teachers. I learn more about life and love from my kids than everyone else I know put together. But Jukie is my master teacher. My Yoda, if you will. As Jukie seeks to express his joy and affection for the people he loves, he teaches me the value of that same connection with others, too. Seems so simple, right? Of course we're here to love and connect – what's the big deal? Yet, ego and feelings complicate relationships. It's easy to get mad at people we love. In fact, it's super easy to get mad at Jukie! His mischievous antics can make a mama crazy. (Thank goodness his fascination with the sound of breaking glass ended years ago.) But, like any kid, Jukie dislikes parental disapproval and meets our looks of displeasure with offerings of apologetic kisses. When I feel annoyed with the behavior of someone I love, I try to remember that the ultimate desire of any close relationship lies in the same connection that Jukie enacts with his wordless gestures. We should all live a bit more like the way Jukie lives. He gives affection easily, forgives quickly, and loves unconditionally.

If it weren't for the memory of others to corroborate my own, I'd almost wonder if I dreamt those years with Jukie; for Talking Jukie feels like a dream, and I'd give everything I own to hear him say "Mama" just one more time.

But as I cannot, I have come to depend upon the loving physicality of our closeness. Jukie says "Mama" to me with his eyes.

The Time of the Rubber Duck

After dark the rubber duck's tail feathers twitch.
After dark the rubber duck grinds its beak.
After dark the rubber duck eyes the cat.
After dark the rubber duck burps.
After dark the rubber duck watches the drip drip drip.
After dark the rubber duck squints at the other toys.
After dark the rubber duck plugs up the drain.
After dark the rubber duck tips the others into the tub.
After dark the rubber duck knocks the soap into the water; it'll be
    mush by dawn.
After dark the rubber duck gooses the cat.
After dark the rubber duck hides the baby's toys under the sink.
After dark the rubber duck whispers evil quacks to the dog.

The rubber duck can't yet open doors.
The rubber duck can't yet climb the bedpost.

Disassemble the Hunchback

First, clearly, the hump, which turned out to be a falsie.
Secondly, the misshapen nose – a prosthetic.
The bulbous eyes were inflated,

as were the neck and the crawling warts and the active boils.
I need the screwdriver, rather than the scalpel for this one.
One shoe was needlessly larger than the other.

His one lift made him stumble and drag his foot like that.
There are so many ways to love this hunchback
now that we know that he was an imposter.

Jukie Life Lessons

One of Davis, California's claims to fame is that there are more PhD's living here than in any other small town in the U.S. In 2006, CNN *Money Magazine* ranked Davis as the second most educated city (in terms of the percentage of residents with graduate degrees) in the United States.

And when I look around at the Farmers' Market each Saturday morning, the population seems to be divided equally between parents and children (and about 30,000 college students). Davis boasts one of the strongest school districts in the state, so it's no surprise that one finds a tremendous local focus on our smart kids. We're like Garrison Keillor's Lake Wobegon where all of the children are above average.

For the most part, living in a town with so many engaged and involved parents is wonderful. (I'm married to a UC Davis PhD.) There is, however, another side to all of that near-obsessive focus on our children's academic lives: it's intense. Kids certainly feel this pressure to perform to their parents' high expectations. And parents feel the competition among each other.

I have overheard many typical Davis conversations over the years featuring parents of preschoolers who wonder which path might take their child to an Ivy League school, or who agonize over whether or not to place their child in a self-contained GATE classroom (gifted and talented education).

Truthfully, I have been involved with some of these discussions. I also struggle with finding the right balance between obsessing over a child's academic performance versus providing support while following a child's lead.

Perhaps I have an edge that others don't. For when I find myself wondering if my twelve-year-old daughter will get into Stanford, her nine-year-old brother, Jukie, quickly slaps me squarely into reality. Jukie won't be going to Stanford, or to UC Davis, or to any university. And, truly, none of that matters, as I'm often struck by this simple truth: Jukie is the wisest person I know. He has many life lessons to teach the rest of us.

His lessons aren't taught at any school. Those who are privileged to know Jukie will learn just by spending time with my boy.

Start each day anew, with a clean slate. Jukie doesn't know from grudges. He doesn't hold onto anger. Of course, like the rest of us, he sometimes feels anger. And he has no problem communicating his anger. Occasionally, Jukie bites or pinches to show us his displeasure, usually over complying with a request from Mom or Dad. However, his anger subsides within seconds. He apologizes to us by grabbing our hands and giving us about ten kisses.

Judge not. Imagine a world where none of the "ism's" existed. As far as I can tell, the only criterion that Jukie uses to judge a person is kindness.

If you're happy and you know it, let everyone know. Jukie is pure joy. He couldn't care less whether or not expressing his joy (loudly) is appropriate. When the boy is moved to laugh, he laughs uproariously. Soon, everyone around him joins in laughing; his bliss is infectious. And just try worrying about anything while you're engaged in raucous laughter. Often when Jukie starts to laugh like that, I forget even what I had been doing.

It's the little things. Jukie can spend hours examining the plants in our backyard. Through Jukie's eyes, I see the beauty in each jasmine flower. Lying on our backs on Jukie's trampoline, Jukie and I notice the pattern of clouds above. Through Jukie's delight, I remember the thrill of spinning on a tire swing. As he plays with my wedding rings, I take a moment to recall the day I got married, and kiss the top of Jukie's sweet head. (I had no idea what life held all those years ago.)

Slow down. Everyone who knows Jukie knows how fast he is – the boy can run. But he has another speed. When he's focused on the minute details of his world, his movement comes to a near halt. As I'm frantically doing dishes and laundry and cooking dinner, I often look out to the backyard to find Jukie sitting quietly, thinking. When I'm able, I follow Jukie's lead and slow down. When his sister was a toddler, she used to say, "Mommy, let's be. Let's just be." Jukie reminds me to just be.

Words are overrated. Although Jukie has made great strides using his Picture Exchange Communication System, most of our communication takes place intuitively. Expert at sensing the feelings of others around him, Jukie usually knows exactly what's going on. If the mood in the room is tense, Jukie will start to cry. If those around him are content, Jukie feels content. He is like a human barometer. Other than asking him to stop doing half the stuff he's doing, and trying to get him to do what we want him to do, we mostly communicate our love and affection to and for Jukie. Certainly no child has ever received more hugs and kisses than he.

Expose yourself. Those who know Jukie know that he routinely exposes himself in a multitude of ways. Although he knows the rules dictate otherwise, Jukie enjoys taking off all of his clothes. He removes his pants any time he feels like it. Fortunately, his brother and sister police this behavior. "Jukie, put your pants back on" is overheard frequently in our backyard. Lately, though, I've been thinking about the way in which Jukie has exposed himself to us on a deeper level. Because Jukie wears no social mask, neither do the rest of us. When we are with our boy, all eyes look our way. I have learned the liberation that comes from dispensing with one's public face. Once that façade is removed, we're left without pretense. I no longer try to appear to be anything. Why bother? I sometimes feel like Jukie and I are both saying, "Here I am, world!"

Never pass an opportunity to dance. Like the rest of us, Jukie hears music in his head. The difference is that he acts on it. There's no stopping Jukie when he is moved to dance or to spin or to jump. Seeing the joy in his face, no one would want to stop him. Anyone traveling through Davis may encounter a cute little redhead and his mom dancing around the parks.

The White House belongs to everyone. For the most part, Jukie is met with kindness and interest by strangers he encounters. However, sometimes, I get the feeling that people wish a kid like Jukie weren't taken everywhere. We've gotten the "look" at the movie theater, art galleries, and restaurants. And this is where the mama bear in me rises up. Jukie has the right to go anywhere the rest of us go. Surprisingly, he often behaves better than other kids. A while back while visiting Washington DC my own daughter suggested that Jukie might not be allowed to enter The White House, asking, "Mom, is Jukie allowed in The White House??" Pretending that I didn't know why she was concerned, I responded, "Why not – they have his social security number, just like the rest of us." If I were to keep Jukie out of any potentially challenging situation, he'd never go anywhere. How will he learn to behave appropriately if not given the chance? And how will those who are not fortunate enough to know a kid like Jukie learn to appreciate him and others like him? (For the record, Jukie did pull a few Jukie-stunts in George Bush's White House. I'm sure he'd have been much better behaved had we visited during Obama's tenure.)

Take care of each other. Because Jukie needs more care than most, Jukie's brother and sister are learning an invaluable lesson: we all take care of and look out for one another. They learn kindness and empathy way beyond their years. Such a gift.

Other obligations can wait when there's fun to be had. Just when I think I know how I am going to spend my morning, Jukie will grab my hand and drag me in the other direction. Jukie is always in the moment. And I never regret following him.

Life is about love. A great misconception about people with autism is that they don't connect with others. In truth, they do connect; it just looks different. And, in fact, Jukie's single greatest goal each day is to be with the people he loves. He kisses our arms and stomachs constantly. He wants to be held and tickled. As I tuck him in bed each night, the sweetest part of my day, he pulls me close, grabs my arms, wrapping them around him. Kissing his sweet, soft cheek, I silently thank him for everything he gave me that day.

After the Sermon

Deciphering his body next to a girl
in the fourth pew, and comparing
Leviticus to musical Dante,
he felt expirations of sensory discovery,
the new pain of possibility,
and the simultaneous dry warmth
of cold, promised, perpetual flame.
Puberty wrapped up in causality,
hot blood seeking to emerge,
trying in public not to exclaim
his angry love to a freckled shoulder
beneath a firmament of orange dress –
brokering the fight between
ostentation and shrill despair.

Sleeping in a Field of Un-

– after Shakespeare's "Sonnet 13"

Exempted from ownership,
you are sweetly unaware of endings.
Yours is a semblance of life.

Do you belong to yourself?
Stormy gusts provoke no thoughts
of unanticipated husbandry,

no thoughts of the deceased,
or even the act of deceasing.
The tree's branch, a thousand patterns.

Unwrinkled, uncreased, unencumbered,
unprepared: so much "un" –
The absences pile up in your silence.

My dear love, I am your father.
Like you, your son will never say so.

DR. ANDY JONES is a poet, MC, faculty member at UC Davis, radio talk show host, public speaker, social media consultant, and essayist. Andy has taught writing and literature classes at the University of California, Davis since 1990, and since 2000 has hosted "Dr. Andy's Poetry and Technology Hour" on radio station KDVS, Wednesday afternoons at 5:00 P.M. (see poetrytechnology.com). Among the 1,000 guests he has interviewed on the radio show are Sherman Alexie, Margaret Atwood, T.C. Boyle, Chris Brogan, Stephen Dunn, John Lescroart, Ralph Nader, and Gary Snyder. His poems have appeared in many small journals and newspapers, including *Poetry Digest, Epicenter, A Light Left On, The Homestead Review, Snakeskin, The Blue Moon Literary and Art Review, The Oddity,* and *The Sacramento News and Review.* Andy hosts and coordinates the bimonthly Poetry Night Reading Series at the John Natsoulas Gallery in Davis (see poetryindavis.com). His recent projects include co-authoring a book of poetry, *Split Stock,* with Brad Henderson, and founding a web design and social media consultancy called Eager Mondays, LLC. Find Andy on the web at andyojones.com and at twitter.com/andyojones.

KATE DUREN is an essayist, blogger, a *Bringing Baby Home Certified Gottman Educator* for couples, and a coach for new parents. The Director of Media Relations for the Smith-Lemli-Opitz Foundation, Kate works to support parents, coordinate communication and collaboration among parents of children with Smith-Lemli-Opitz syndrome, and raise money for medical research. Author of the blog Thriving in

Holland (at kateduren.blogspot.com), Kate also runs "Help for New Moms," a new mom consultancy at helpfornewmoms.com. Originally from Chicago, Kate lives in Davis, California with her husband, Andy, and their three children, Geneva, Jukie, and Truman. Find Kate online at twitter.com/kateduren.

 **JACKSON "JUKIE" DUREN** was born in January 2001 with Smith-Lemli-Opitz syndrome, a rare metabolic and developmental disorder that makes it difficult for those with it to metabolize cholesterol. In addition, Jukie has what is called regressive autism, meaning that he started to lose skills and language when he was about two years old. Today Jukie is curious, energetic, often patient, and affectionate, as well as entirely non-verbal. Although Smith-Lemli-Opitz syndrome affects only about one in 50,000 newborns, medical research into SLO continues, supported in part by funds raised by the Smith-Lemli-Opitz Foundation (see www.smithlemliopitz.org).

All profits from the sales of the book Where's Jukie? *will be donated to the Smith-Lemli-Opitz Foundation to fund medical research into the causes, treatment, and understanding of Smith-Lemli-Opitz syndrome.*

Smith–Lemli–Opitz/RSH Foundation
c/o Gretchen Noah
P.O. Box 10598
Fargo, ND 58106
USA

E-mail: gnoah@smithlemliopitz.org

Web: www.smithlemliopitz.org/donations/

A Note on *Where's Jukie?*

The poems and essays in *Where's Jukie?* are set in Goudy Old Style typeface, a font created by Frederic W. Goudy in 1915 on behalf of the American Type Founders. It was the twenty-fifth typeface created by Goudy and is considered among the most readable and enduring typefaces ever produced.

Book Design: Evan White, Absurd Publications

© Absurd Publications